F-4 PHANTOM

FRANK B. MORMILLO

LONDON

IAN ALLAN LTD

First published 1990

ISBN 0 7110 1928 2

Published by Ian Allan Ltd, Shepperton, Surrey; and printed by Ian Allan Printing Ltd at their works at Coombelands in Runnymede, England

Previous page:
The last active duty conventional USAF Phantom fighter-bomber wing, the 4th TFW at Seymour-Johnson AFB, NC, began conversion to the F-15E Strike Eagle in December 1988. This F-4E, assigned to the 4th TFW CO, was photographed taking off from the Tactical Fighter Weapons Center (TFWC) at Nellis AFB, Nv during the Gunsmoke '85 competition.
Frank B. Mormillo
Right:
Some of the most dramatic photos of tactical aircraft are taken from air refuelling tankers. This 114th TFTS F-4C was photographed while tanking from a 452nd AREFW KC-10 Extender during an inter-service exercise known as 'Lobo Flag' which was hosted by VFA-305 (USNR) at NAS Point Mugu, Ca, in August 1988.
Frank B. Mormillo

PREFACE

This volume is not a definitive study of the McDonnell Douglas F-4 Phantom II. After more than three decades of operational service, the Phantom still remains a viable combat aeroplane and, barring dramatic force reductions for either political or fiscal considerations, will continue in service for many years yet. Consequently, it will probably be up to some photo-journalist from the next generation to produce a definitive study that, in all likelihood, will turn out to be a massive undertaking.

Instead, this book is basically a photo album illustrating, as much as possible, the Phantom in its most recent service worldwide. All of the photos included in this album were taken during the present decade, with most having been taken during the past two or three years. Although this volume is not as complete as I would have liked because of my inability to obtain recent photos of Phantoms from all of the aeroplane's operators, I hope that the readers will still find this to be a worthwhile and fresh presentation.

With the make-up of the US Phantom force in particular being in something of a state of rapid change these days, many of the photos in this album cannot be repeated. In fact, some of the Phantoms illustrated will already have been withdrawn from service by the time that this book is published and in the hands of its readers.

Frank B. Mormillo
Covina, California
USA
1989

Sole distributors for the USA

Motorbooks International
Publishers & Wholesalers Inc
Osceola, Wisconsin 54020, USA ®

Acknowledgements

Although I have produced and illustrated many articles about military aviation, this is my very first book project and its completion would not have been possible without the gracious help of many individuals and organisations. In particular, I would like to thank Andrew Farrow, Publishing Manager at Ian Allan Ltd, for having confidence in my ability to undertake this task.

A special note of appreciation is due to the 452nd AREFW (AFRES), the 22nd AREFW (SAC) and VMGR-352 (USMC) for allowing me to use their tanker aircraft as photo platforms in a project that essentially gives media coverage to aircraft from other commands and units. Even more heartfelt thanks are due to Capt Steve Brennan (USMC) and Lt-Col Tony Scheuller (ANG) who gave me rides and excellent photo opportunities in VMFA-134 F-4S and 152nd TRG RF-4C Phantoms.

Many photographers provided such excellent selections of photos illustrating Phantoms in worldwide service that it was extremely difficult to edit them down to a final selection. These include: Diethard Achterberg, Peter R. Foster, Theo W. van Geffen, Robbie Shaw, Herman J. Sixma and Katsuhiko Tokunaga.

The following individuals (listed in alphabetical order) provided additional photos and photo opportunities that were essential to the production of this volume: Maj Victor J. Andrijaukas (USAF), TFWC PAO; Lt Kevin Baggett (USAF), TAC PAO; Lt-Col Donald L. Black (USAF), TAC PAO; Lt Michelle DeWerth (USAF), George AFB PAO; Maj Ronald D. Fuchs (USAF), Western Region PAO; Don Haley, AFFTC PAO; Cdr Phil Hazelrig (USN), CVWR-30 CO; Brig-Gen David C. Henley, Nevada National Guard Reserve; Kesaharu Imai, Publisher, Bunrindo Co Ltd; SSgt Richard Kennelly (USMC), MAG-46; Sgt Anne Larsen (USMC), MAG-46, PAO; Maj Larry Matlock (ANG), 152nd TRG; Ichiro Mitsui, Editor, the KOKU-FAN; TSgt Sharon Naimo, AFRES PAO; MSgt Bill Nicoletti (ANG), 163rd TFG PAO; Lt-Col Fred C. Peck (USMC), Headquarters Marine Corps PAO; Patricia Price, Tracor Flight Systems; Maj Suzanne Randle (USAF), SAC PAO; Lt-Col Harold L. Rothgeb, Jr (USAF), Department of the Air Force PAO; Capt A. V. Stephenson (USAF), 22nd AREFW PAO; Capt Richard Williamson (AFRES), 452nd AREFW PAO; and Col Niles E. Vanderhoof, Nevada ANG.

Other photos and additional assistance also came from: Air Attaché, Embassy of the Federal Republic of Germany, Washington DC; Col Eugenio Jack Follá, Air Attaché to the Embassy of Spain, Washington DC; and Brig-Gen Vural Sezer, Defence and Air Attaché, Turkish Embassy, Washington DC.

Right:
The specialised F-4G *Wild Weasel* version of the Phantom will probably remain in service with the USAF until the turn of the century. Flying near the wing's home station, George AFB, Ca, are the F-4Gs assigned to the CO of the 37th TFW and the COs of his three squadrons, the 561st, 562nd and 563rd TFS. These *Wild Weasels* are armed with AGM-45A Shrike, AGM-65 Maverick and AGM-88A HARM air-to-ground missiles, AIM-7 Sparrow air-to-air missiles and cluster bombs. *USAF*

Front cover:
The 196th TFS, 163rd TFG operated F-4C Phantoms from March AFB, Ca until it re-equipped with F-4Es. Part of the California ANG, the unit was slated to become a Tactical Air Support Squadron with 0A-10A Thunderbolts during FY 1990. However, after appeals from squadron personnel and a local congressman, that decision was changed and the unit will now become a reconnaissance squadron with RF-4Cs. This 163rd TFG F-4C was photographed from a 22nd AREFW KC-135 Stratotanker over the Grand Canyon in Arizona. *Frank B. Mormillo*

Back cover:
This colourfully-marked, shark-nosed JASDF F-4EJ is assigned to 306 Hikotai at Komatsu AB. The red and yellow stars on the air intake splitter vane probably indicates successful interceptions of Soviet aircraft over the Sea of Japan.
Katsuhiko Tokunaga/KOKU-FAN

F-4 PHANTOM

Now in its fourth decade of service, the McDonnell Douglas F-4 Phantom II must certainly be rated as one of the most successful combat aircraft of all time. Originally conceived under the designation F3H-G as a single-seat, twin-engined development of the F3H Demon, the basic Phantom design lost out to the Chance Vought F-8U Crusader in a 1953 competition to provide the US Navy (USN) with a new multi-mission aeroplane and underwent several changes before it finally emerged from the McDonnell plant in St Louis, Missouri as the F4H-1 in May 1958.

After the initial rejection, revised design studies soon resulted in a proposed Phantom capable of Mach 1.5, designated YAH-1, that would have been powered by Wright J65 Sapphire engines, armed with four 20mm cannon and Sparrow air-to-air missiles and capable of carrying a wide variety of air-to-ground ordnance on 11 external hardpoints. However, the design was soon revised once again to include more powerful General Electric J79 engines, fewer external hardpoints and an all-missile air-to-air armament. After inspecting single and two-seat proposals, the Navy finalised the design as a two-seat fleet defence interceptor under the designation F4H-1.

When the F4H-1 prototype emerged from the factory, few at that time could have realised that the massive 56,000lb fighter with its bent-up wingtips and drooping horizontal tail surfaces would eventually prove to be one of the best warplanes of its era, see service into the 21st century and, in terms of numbers, probably be the most important Western supersonic tactical fighter-bomber of the 20th century. By the time that Phantom production was brought to a halt in 1981, 5,195 F-4s had been built in 17 major variants for use by a dozen air forces around the world. At least 5,057 Phantoms were built in St Louis (there are some reports that an additional half-dozen or so RF-4Es were built in St Louis after completion of the 5,057th Phantom which has been officially listed as the last US-built F-4) and the rest were built by Mitsubishi in Japan.

Although the Phantom was initially a Navy design, it soon became the standard fighter-bomber for the US Marine Corps (USMC) and US Air Force (USAF) as well. In fact, in the long term, the USAF actually became the biggest user of the aeroplane and will be the last of the three US armed services to retain Phantoms in operational service.

Though impressive at first sight, many considered the Phantom to be a very ugly aeroplane. In fact, some even referred to it as 'The Big Ugly' and stated that its design was proof of the concept that 'with enough power, even a brick can fly'. Yet, ugly or not, the F-4 soon proved to be an outstanding aeroplane, lending some credence to the phrase 'beauty is as beauty does'. USN and USMC pilots wasted little time flying Phantoms in a series of world record performances.

On 6 December 1959, USN Cdr Lawrence E. Flint Jr flew a YF4H-1 prototype on a mission called Operation 'Top Flight' to a peak altitude of 98,557ft and, on 5 September 1960, USMC Lt-Col Thomas H. Miller flew a Navy F4H-1 (later designated F-4A) around a 500km closed course at an average speed of 1,216.76mph. On 25 September 1960, USN Cdr J. F. Davis flew a Phantom around a 100km closed circuit at an average speed of

Far right:
Under the ideal blue skies of southern California, this 37th TFW maintenance technician is securing a Maverick-armed 562nd TFS F-4G *Wild Weasel* after a mission over the Mojave Desert. *Frank B. Mormillo*

1,390.24mph. A trans-continental record was set on 24 May 1961 when an operational USN crew consisting of Lt R. F. Gordon and Lt B. R. Young flew an F-4B from California to New York in 2hr 49min 9.9sec, averaging over 896mph for the 2,446-mile flight. Flying an F-4A named *Sageburner*, USN Lt Huntington Hardisty and Lt Earl H. DeEsch set a 3km low-altitude record on 28 August 1961 by averaging 902.769mph during four runs over the course while keeping the aeroplane between 125-175ft above the ground. Probably the Phantom's most impressive record of all was set by USMC Lt-Col Robert B. Robinson on 22 November 1961 when he flew an F-4A named *Skyburner* at an average speed of 1,606.3mph during two runs over a 15/25km course at 45,000ft while keeping his altitude to within 100m from the start to finish gates. On 5 December 1961, USN Cdr George W. Ellis set a sustained altitude record of 66,443.8ft in a Phantom and, in early 1962, under the project name 'High Jump', USN pilots from the Operational Test and Evaluation Force flew a series of missions that broke every existing time-to-climb record, actually exceeding the 'Top Flight' mark with a peak altitude of over 100,000ft during the time-to-30,000m effort.

Over the years, the basic Phantom shape has not changed a great deal. The initial batch of development aircraft did feature a fairly low profile cockpit canopy and relatively small nose radome which were both changed on the 19th development aeroplane, a YF4H-1. From that point on, visibility for the aircrew was improved by raising the cockpit several inches and bulging the canopy while the radome was enlarged to accommodate a 32in radar dish antenna in place of the previous 24in dish.

When the USAF decided to obtain a reconnaissance model of the Phantom — designated RF-4C — terrain mapping radar, side-looking aircraft radar and various camera systems replaced the offensive weapons systems and radar mounted in a more slender nose that was extended by 33in. Later on, when the USAF realised that it would be a good idea to include a built-in gun for close-in air-to-air combat, the nose of the F-4E model was redesigned to accommodate a 20mm Vulcan cannon and an improved solid-state radar with a smaller dish, resulting in an even more streamlined and longer nose. Furthermore, when Britain selected the Phantom for use by the RN and RAF and decided essentially to mate the USN F-4J airframe with Rolls-Royce Spey engines, a few more subtle changes did appear. Since the Spey engine is larger in diameter than the J79, British Phantoms featured deeper aft fuselages in the engine bay area and required enlarged air intakes.

Other changes to the basic Phantom profile, though important with regard to certain aspects of various missions, did relatively little to change the overall appearance of the aeroplane, centring mainly around the disposition of various ECM antennas, bulged wheel-wells for land-based models, slotted leading edges on the stabilators, leading edge manoeuvring slats on the wings of some models and built-in TISEO (Target Identification System-Electro Optical) pods on the left wing of some F-4Es.

The basic Phantom models produced for the USN and USMC were: F-4A (F4H-1), F-4B, RF-4B (USMC only), F-4J, F-4N and F-4S. The F-4N and F-4S were basically refurbished B and J models. In addition, the Navy also operated a dozen F-4Gs (not related to the USAF *Wild Weasel* F-4G) for a while which were essentially F-4Bs fitted with air-to-ground data link equipment; those aircraft were eventually converted to standard F-4B configuration as were a number of TF-4A trainers. Special USN variants modified from standard production aircraft included DF-4B drone controllers and QF-4B drones.

USAF models of the Phantom included the F-4C (initially designated F-110A), F-4D, F-4E, F-4G and RF-4C. The F-4G *Wild Weasels* are actually converted F-4Es intended for the specialised SAM suppression role. Fitted with revised avionics for that mission, the primary external differences between the E and G models includes the location of podded RHAW (Radar Homing and Warning) antennae on top of the vertical fin and the replacement of the built-in 20mm gun with antennae and receivers in a slightly larger under-nose pod.

Other Phantom models produced included: F-4EJ, licence-built in Japan for the JASDF with the inflight refuelling system and bombing equipment deleted and the JASDF RF-4EJ reconnaissance fighter; F-4F, basically the F-4E without the boundary layer control system, leading edge flaps and Sparrow missile capability for the Luftwaffe; RF-4E built as a reconnaissance fighter for foreign air forces; and the Royal Navy F-4K (FG-1) and RAF F-4M (FGR-2). When the RAF later obtained 15 additional Phantoms in 1983 (ex-USN F-4J models), those aircraft were given the designation F Mk 3.

In addition to US and British service, Phantoms have also been operated by: Australia (24 F-4Es and RF-4Es leased for a

Far left:
Despite the WW tailcode, this F-4E was not assigned to the 37th TFW when the photo was taken from a 452nd AREFW KC-10 in February 1989. The Phantom in question had been retired recently from service with the 51st TFW at Osan, Korea and was over the Pacific Ocean en route to Hill AFB, Ut, for conversion to the F-4G configuration. The 51st TFW painted the WW code on the tail to indicate the aeroplane's next assignment.
Capt Richard Williamson/AFRES

Far right:
Until replaced by F-16C Fighting Falcons, 52nd TFW F-4E fighter-bombers at Spangdahlem AB, West Germany, teamed up with the wing's F-4G *Wild Weasels* for SAM suppression missions. The wing now operates F-4G/F-16C SAM suppression teams. *Herman J. Sixma/IAAP*

few years pending the delivery of F-111C strike fighters and returned to the US by 1974); Egypt (F-4Es); Federal Republic of Germany (F-4Fs and RF-4Es); Greece (F-4Es and RF-4Es); Iran (F-4Ds, F-4Es and RF-4Es); Israel (F-4Es and RF-4Es); Japan (F-4EJs and RF-4EJs); South Korea (F-4Ds and F-4Es); Spain (F-4Cs and RF-4Cs); and Turkey (F-4Es and RF-4Es).

Although several other countries, particularly in Latin America, had also expressed an interest in Phantoms, US State Department guidelines regarding the sale of sophisticated weapons to some Third World areas restricted the procurement of F-4s by those countries.

During more than 30 years of service, the F-4 Phantom has distinguished itself in battle repeatedly. It bore the brunt of USAF, USN and USMC air combat operations in South East Asia for many years and was the mount of the only US aces of the Vietnam War. Phantoms have also been used with telling effect by Israel in its Middle East conflicts and were blooded in combat by Iran in the war against Iraq. Two NATO allies, Greece and Turkey, even flew Phantoms against each other during the conflict over Cyprus in 1974.

Yet, after all of those years and in spite of the appearance of new designs, the Phantom still remains a viable and effective frontline combat aeroplane. Few new combat aircraft can still match the Phantom's ability to carry up to 16,000lb of external ordnance for air-to-ground missions or a combination of four heat-seeking and four radar-guided missiles (in addition to the built-in gun in the E model), together with external fuel tanks, for the air-to-air mission. Furthermore, there is actually very little difference in top speed and range between the Phantom and some of its intended successors.

While it is true that recent combat experience has placed more emphasis on manoeuvrability and acceleration, past experience would seem to indicate that sheer speed can also play an important part in air-to-air combat, especially when used to its best advantage by experienced aircrews. In actual fact, there is still a lot of life left in the venerable Phantom. Though Phantoms have already disappeared from frontline and reserve USN squadrons and are rapidly leaving the ranks of USMC and USAF tactical fighter-bomber squadrons, USMC RF-4Bs will probably continue flying the Corps' reconnaissance mission until the mid-1990s. F-4G *Wild Weasels*, together with RF-4C reconnaissance Phantoms may remain in service with the USAF and its reserve components until the turn of the century. In all likelihood, Phantoms will probably continue to render valuable service overseas well into the next century! Though basic overhaul costs alone are actually close to or in excess of the original purchase price of Phantoms, the cost of new-generation fighter-bombers is now so astronomical that it is hard to see how some air forces will be able to afford alternatives. Furthermore, partly because of its size and robust structure, the Phantom still has some growth potential.

Germany and Japan have already instituted avionics upgrades and structural reinforcements that will keep their aircraft operational for another decade, while Israel is actually trying to market upgrade packages, under the appellation Phantom 2000, that could keep the aeroplane viable beyond the turn of the century. Although, in the interest of economy, Israel itself has apparently opted to concentrate on avionics upgrades and structural strengthening for its own Phantoms, the proposed packages could also include new engines, conformal fuel tanks and canard control surfaces on the shoulders of the air intakes.

Even the USAF has shown an interest in such upgrades, having awarded the Boeing Military Airplane Company a contract to develop such packages for possible sale to friendly foreign countries. If taken to its full potential, a total upgrade package, including replacement of the J79 engines with new-generation Pratt & Whitney PW1120 engines, would provide avionics suites comparable to those in the newest combat aircraft; a reduction in empty weight of nearly a ton; almost a three-ton increase in total thrust from engines that burn less fuel; and a significant increase in total fuel capacity.

The engine change alone is calculated to provide a 27% increase in acceleration from Mach 0.6 to Mach 1.2 at 20,000ft and an 18% increase from Mach 0.9 to Mach 1.6 at 30,000ft. In addition, turn rate should improve by about 13%, low level penetration speed could be increased by up to 50kt and take-off roll could be reduced by about 21%. The overall weight reduction, in conjunction with the increased power, could provide an increased ordnance capability in the region of two tons and the reduction in fuel consumption, together with the ability to carry additional fuel, could increase the Phantoms' operational radius by about 40%.

Below:
Like many other Phantom units, the 35th TTW at George AFB, Ca, is in the process of changing colour schemes. Until all of the aircraft assigned go through overhaul and are repainted, it has F-4E Phantoms in both the European One camouflage scheme and the Compass Ghost Gray scheme. This photo was taken from a 452nd AREFW KC-10 in June 1989.
Frank B. Mormillo

Far right:
Assigned to the 35th TTW, the 20th TFTS is tasked primarily to train German aircrews over the ranges of the southwestern US where the weather is seldom unfit for flying.
Frank B. Mormillo

Naturally, as the Israelis have already discovered, a total upgrade would be fairly expensive — up to $11 million per aeroplane. However, although that is much more than the original purchase price of new Phantoms (it reportedly varied between $2.8 million and $3.5 million per aircraft during the Vietnam War) it is still a lot less than the cost of many new fighter-bombers, some of which go for $30-40 million per unit.

Yet, in spite of the potential benefits of a total upgrade package, there seems to be a reluctance to go that route by some of the major Phantom operators. In all likelihood, there is probably a deep-seated desire by many to get the newest product available regardless of cost. When the subject was brought up with one US Phantom pilot, his response was: 'That would probably be OK for some Third World countries, but it wouldn't be good for us. The airplane simply requires too much maintenance at this stage of its life.' However, it would seem logical that a total upgrade of engines, avionics, flight control systems and structure might actually lower the Phantom's maintenance requirements.

As is often the case when venerable combat aircraft begin to enter the retirement process, there are many gatherings to celebrate stories of past exploits and frequent mutterings of phrases such as 'Phabulous Phantoms Phorever'. However, in the case of the Phantom, the emotion doesn't seem to be very deep. When aeroplanes such as the F-105 Thunderchief and F-106 Delta Dart were retired, the pilots were almost on the verge of tears. In fact, at one F-105 retirement ceremony/Thud driver reunion, one of the F-105 pilots spotted an old friend from the days of squadron service and asked him what he was flying at the time. Looking wistfully at one of the remaining F-105s, the pilot replied: 'I'm flying two-seat, multi-engined bombers'. He was referring to the F-4 Phantom.

Indeed, the only aircrewmen who seem to show any real emotion at Phantom retirements are the non-pilot-rated NFOs and WSOs who will have to find new jobs because single-seat aeroplanes like the F-16 Fighting Falcon and F/A-18 Hornet are replacing the Phantoms in many units.

In a nutshell this is the reason why perhaps, after years of sterling service and with seemingly much more yet to give, most fighter pilots aren't that sad to see the Phantoms go. In spite of the apparent advantages of a second crewman to reduce the workload and keep an extra set of eyes open for 'bandits', most fighter pilots are really lone wolves at heart and, fabulous as it may be, the F-4 Phantom is really a big two-seater that pilots find hard to get emotional over.

From the manufacturer's standpoint, it is obvious that it would be more profitable to produce new designs than to upgrade older aircraft. In fact, it was rumoured that, when McDonnell Douglas brought the Phantom production line to a close, there was still some sales potential left in the design; however, the company didn't want the old fighter to compete with its newer designs. Even more revealing is the report that development of an uprated reconnaissance Phantom for Israel which, with modified air intakes and provision for pre-compressor section cooling (water injection), would have been able to cruise at Mach 2.4 for 10min was dropped in 1975 partly out of concern for the possible effect that the aircraft (designated RF-4X) might have had on F-15 Eagle funding.

Although it may be getting on in years and lacking some of the glamour of its intended successors, the 'Phabulous Phantom' may still stay around long enough to outlast some of these successors!

Carrying special tail markings for the RAM '86 competition, this 1st TRS, 18th TFW RF-4C was photographed at Kadena AB, Okinawa in late 1986.
Robbie Shaw

Although the last RF-4C came off the production line in January 1974, this version of the Phantom is destined to remain in service as the USAF's primary tactical reconnaissance fighter until the end of the century. When photographed in September 1985, this RF-4C was in service with the 10th TRW at RAF Alconbury. *Peter R. Foster*

Assigned to the 67th TRW, Bergstrom AFB, Tx, this RF-4C was
photographed blasting off from the TFWC runway at Nellis AFB during a
'Red Flag' exercise. *Frank B. Mormillo*

Known as the 'High Rollers' in deference to Nevada's legalised gambling industry, the 192nd TRS (ANG) operates 22 RF-4C Phantoms at the Reno Cannon IAP as a part of the 152nd TRG.
Frank B. Mormillo

Although US reconnaissance squadrons tend to associate with the phrase 'alone, unarmed and unafraid', 152nd TRG RF-4Cs can frequently be seen flying in formations of four or more aeroplanes during peacetime training missions over the nearby ranges at NAS Fallon, Nv. The reconnaissance Phantoms are also wired to accept Sidewinder missiles for self-defence, but that capability is not used at present.
Frank B. Mormillo

Photographed shortly before the unit converted to F-4Es, this 163rd TFG (California ANG) F-4C was landing at March AFB, Ca after aborting a bombing practice mission because of a generator failure. The F-4's emergency ram-air turbine can be easily seen in the extended position, practice bombs are still on the racks and the braking chute has just started to deploy. *Frank B. Mormillo*

F-4Ds from the 148th FIG (Minnesota ANG) and the 144th FIW (California ANG) flew training missions as part of Det 11, ANG Support Center, from Ramstein AB, West Germany, in March 1987. Most Air Defence ANG Phantoms are destined to be replaced by F-16A Fighting Falcons.

Theo W. van Geffen/IAAP

Det 11 F-4D ANG operational training missions conducted from Ramstein AB in March 1987 included navigation training and in-flight refuelling from SAC KC-135A Stratotankers.
Theo W. van Geffen/IAAP

Far left:
The 114th TFTS (ANG) is an RTU (Replacement Training Unit) at Kingsley Field, Or. Showing off the 'Black Hawk' markings on its drop tank, this 114th TFTS F-4C was photographed breaking away from a 22nd AREFW KC-10 tanker during a 'Lobo Flag' exercise over the Mojave Desert of southern California.
Frank B. Mormillo

Left:
Together with the 114th TFTS, the 123rd FIS is part of the Oregon ANG's 142nd FIG. Operating from the Portland International Airport, the 123rd FIS flew low-visibility grey-camouflaged F-4Cs for interceptor missions before converting to F-16A Fighting Falcons in 1989.
Frank B. Mormillo

Sporting immaculate grey tactical camouflage schemes, these 924th TFG (AFRES) F-4Ds from Bergstrom AFB, Tx, were preparing to take-off from Nellis AFB, Nv, for a Gunsmoke '87 bombing mission. The aircraft are armed with 25lb practice bombs and SUU-23/A gunpods, and used AN/ASQ-153 'Pave Spike' laser designating pods under the forward Sparrow missile bay to improve bombing accuracy. *Frank B. Mormillo*

Armed with 25lb practice bombs and an SUU-23/A gunpod, this 187th TFG F-4D from Dannelly Field, Al, was taking-off from Nellis AFB, Nv, for a Gunsmoke '87 bombing competition mission when this photo was taken. *Frank B. Mormillo*

Right:

The 188th TFG (ANG) from Fort Smith, Ar, brought beautifully finished F-4Cs to Nellis AFB, Nv, for the Gunsmoke '85 bombing competition. These 188th TFG ordnance technicians were taking part in a 'Loadeo' — a weapons loading competition in which they were graded for speed and safety considerations while loading 500lb bombs on their aircraft. *Frank B. Mormillo*

Far right:

The F-4 Phantom has the distinction of having been the only aircraft that was operated by both the USAF Thunderbirds and the USN Blue Angels flight demonstration teams. When the Thunderbirds retired their F-4Es, the aeroplanes were turned over to the 6512th Test Operations Squadron at the Air Force Flight Test Center, Edwards AFB, Ca, where the survivors still serve alongside similarly-painted white and red F-4Cs, F-4Ds and RF-4Cs. *Frank B. Mormillo*

6512th Test Ops F-4s are used for chase, test support, proficiency training and Test Pilot School training missions at Edwards AFB. From time to time, the Phantoms are also fitted with added systems and used as test planes themselves. This F-4C was fitted with a special nose probe at the AFFTC. *Frank B. Mormillo*

F-4C Phantom 63-7407 is one of the oldest Phantoms still flying. It was used at Edwards AFB for the original Phantom Category Two Systems testing before moving on to operational units. Now back at the AFFTC in its twilight years, 63-7407 is the oldest F-4 at Edwards and still has a few useful years left. AFFTC Phantoms will be replaced by F-15 Eagles and F-16 Fighting Falcons, one at a time, during the next 10 years.

TSgt Larry Long/USAF

Right:
Carrying the civil registration N420FS, this ex-163rd TFG F-4C is operated by Tracor Flight Systems at the Mojave Airport, Ca, for a variety of test operations. Seen taking-off on a mission with a cine camera pod under the left wing and a custom-built stores dispenser (also containing an aft-facing video camera) under the right wing, the aeroplane is actually leased from the Department of Defense and is usually flown on government or aerospace industry contract programmes.
Frank B. Mormillo

Far right:
The survivors of the 46 RF-4Bs built are operated by the USMC's only tactical reconnaissance squadron, VMFP-3 at MCAS El Toro, Ca. Photographed in March 1983, these VMFP-3 RF-4Bs were preparing to embark on the squadron's last deployment aboard the USS *Midway*. Until 1984, the squadron kept a detachment of five RF-4Bs deployed aboard the carrier which is home-ported in Japan. Still the only tactical reconnaissance aircraft in the USMC, VMFP-3's Phantoms will probably remain in service until about 1995. *Frank B. Mormillo*

Active duty USMC F-4S fighter-bombers were all phased out of service in favour of F/A-18 Hornets by the end of FY 1989 and the last USMCR F-4S squadron will make the transition during FY 1993. This VMFA-312 F-4S was photographed while starting out for a Red Flag ACM mission at the TFWC, Nellis AFB, Nv, in January 1985. *Frank B. Mormillo*

VMFA-134 (USMCR) flew its last F-4S missions in December 1988 and became the first Marine Corps Reserve squadron to begin F/A-18 Hornet transition training in January 1989. These VMFA-134 Phantoms were photographed while en route to the Marine Corps Air-Ground Combat Center, Twentynine Palms, Ca, for ACM practice during a Marine Amphibious Brigade Exercise in one of the squadron's last Phantom operations. *Frank B. Mormillo*

Maintenance work continued on VMFA-134 F-4S Phantoms at MCAS El Toro even after the squadron flew its last Phantom operational mission. This F-4S was being repaired after going off the runway sideways at the end of one of the squadron's last Phantom missions. All nine of VMFA-134's F-4S Phantoms were sent to the remaining USMCR F-4S squadrons. *Frank B. Mormillo*

These VMFA-232 F-4S Phantoms from MCAS Kaneohe Bay, Ha, were photographed from a VMGR-352 KC-130 Hercules air refuelling tanker off the coast of southern California during a 'transpac' profile mission required to qualify the aircraft and crews for the trans-Pacific hop back to Hawaii. VMFA-134 later adopted a much more attractive grey tactical camouflage scheme. *Frank B. Mormillo*

Taking part in an ACM training deployment to MCAS El Toro, Ca, this VMFA-232 F-4S and crew were photographed on the VMFA-134 ramp at the start of a mission. VMFA-232 began its transition to the F/A-18 Hornet in FY 1989. *Frank B. Mormillo*

The only F-4 Phantoms still being used by the USN are flying with various test and evaluation units. Flying alongside an F-14 Tomcat, this F-4S from VX-4 is in use at the Pacific Missile Test Center, NAS Point Mugu, Ca. *Frank B. Mormillo*

The Pacific Missile Test Center also operates a number of QF-4B drone conversions. Fully capable of normal piloted operations, the QF-4Bs are flown by remote control when used as targets for missile tests. In most instances, the missiles are programmed to miss the drones by specific distances in order to count as 'hits' and still leave the drones useable for future missions. However, once in a while the drones are targeted for direct hits to test warheads — and sometimes programmed misses actually wind up as direct hits.
Frank B. Mormillo

Left:

This all-white YF-4J Phantom is used for ejection seat tests at the Naval Weapons Center, China Lake, Ca. To facilitate such tests, the cockpit canopy over the backseat is often removed. For reasons of safety, dummies are generally used to simulate aircrewmen for the tests.
Frank B. Mormillo

Assigned to the CO of No 64 Squadron, RAF, this dramatic view of Phantom FGR-2 (F-4M) XT900 clearly shows the deeper aft fuselage engine bay area required to accommodate the Rolls-Royce Spey engines. Most RAF Phantoms have also been fitted with passive warning receivers in fairings on top of the vertical fin. *Robbie Shaw*

Armed with Skyflash and Sidewinder missiles, this No 111 Squadron Phantom FG-1 provides a colourful contrast to the dull, low-visibility colour schemes that seem to characterise many Phantoms today.
Peter R. Foster

No 43 Squadron FG-1 (F-4K) Phantoms maintain a precise echelon
formation over the cloudscape. Originally intended for RN carrier use,
the F-4K has a nose landing gear strut that extends twice as far as the
strut on other Phantom models. Although able to outclimb the
J79-powered Phantoms, the F-4K has a somewhat lower top speed.
Peter R. Foster

Assigned to the CO of No 92 Squadron, this Phantom FGR-2 was photographed while taxying back to the Nellis AFB flightline after a 'Red Flag' mission. The Phantom's long range and aerial refuelling capability make overseas deployments a matter of routine. *Frank B. Mormillo*

No 64 Squadron Phantom FGR-2s are used for RAF Phantom crew conversion at RAF Coningsby by No 228 Operational Conversion Unit (OCU). This pair is carrying finless Sidewinder training missiles on the starboard inner wing racks. *Robbie Shaw*

When the RAF decided to send a squadron of Phantoms to the Falklands after the war with Argentina, it had to turn to the USN for additional F-4s to keep up its NATO commitments. In 1983, 15 F-4S models with smokeless J79-GE-10A engines and standard US fire control systems were ordered and placed into service with No 74 Squadron under the designation Phantom F Mk 3 in 1984. *Robbie Shaw*

This view of a JBG35 Phantom clearly illustrates the underside details of the Luftwaffe F-4F. Though the aeroplane has the wells for AIM-7 Sparrow radar-guided missiles, it is only equipped to use AIM-9 Sidewinder heat-seeking missiles and the built-in 20mm cannon for air-to-air combat. However, the F-4F is likely to be armed eventually with AMRAAM radar-homing missiles as well. *Diethard Achterberg/via IAAP*

Fitted with receptacles for standard USAF boom air refuelling, Luftwaffe F-4F and RF-4E Phantoms have taken increasingly more advantage of that capability within the NATO environment during recent years. These JBG35 F-4Fs were photographed tanking from a USAF SAC 416th BW KC-135A Stratotanker over Sauerland, West Germany.
Diethard Achterberg/via IAAP

Luftwaffe RF-4E Phantoms have been retrofitted with a bombing system and can carry up to 5,000lb of external ordnance for secondary attack missions in addition to their normal reconnaissance role. This AKG52 RF-4E is based at Leck. *Herman J. Sixma/IAAP*

This JBG35 F-4F is carrying an A/A37U Target Tow System which consists of a pod containing an RMU-10/A reel and a TDU-10/B target for gunnery training missions. The target can be reeled away from the tow aeroplane up to a distance of 1,524m. *Diethard Achterberg/via IAAP*

NATO co-operation is well illustrated in this scene which shows a Luftwaffe F-4F from JBG35 flying formation with a Spanish AF F-4C from Escuadrón 122. *Diethard Achterberg/via IAAP*

Right:
Spain has operated two squadrons of F-4C Phantoms out of Torrejon AB since 1974 when three dozen ex-USAF aircraft were supplied under the terms of a defence treaty with the US. Photographed rolling together in the bright Spanish sky, these F-4Cs are assigned to Escuadrón 122.
Spanish AF/via Col Eugenio Jack Follá

Far right:
The Turkish AF operates seven squadrons of F-4E Phantoms for air defence and fighter-bomber missions together with some RF-4Es for long-range all-weather reconnaissance. This 131 FILO (squadron) F-4E is pictured cruising serenely over a Turkish seaside resort.
131 FILO/via IAAP

Phantoms replaced F-100 Super Sabre fighter-bombers and RF-84F
Thunderflash reconnaissance fighters in Turkish service. This 111 FILO
F-4E is seen taxying past a row of derelict RF-84Fs at Eskisehir.
Robbie Shaw

The Greek AF currently operates about 50 F-4Es and eight RF-4Es for air defence and all-weather reconnaissance. This F-4E taxying at Andravida AB is assigned to No 117 Wing which includes Nos 338 and 339 Squadrons. *Herman J. Sixma/IAAP*

F-4E and RF-4E Phantoms have rendered valuable service to the Israeli Defence Force/Air Force in numerous Middle East battles and will be upgraded with new avionics, wiring and strengthened airframes for service up to the turn of the century. This IDF RF-4E was photographed at the IAI aircraft factory near Tel Aviv. *Herman J. Sixma/IAAP*

Having once suffered so much damage from Israeli Phantoms, the Egyptian AF now operates F-4Es as well. The US supplied 35 F-4Es to Egypt after the 1979 Camp David agreement and they now form two air defence/fighter-bomber squadrons under No 222 Wing at Cairo West AB. *Herman J. Sixma/IAAP*

Of all Phantom operators, the Japanese Air Self-Defence Force (JASDF) probably has the most colourful variety. The Phantom is used for air defence and reconnaissance by the JASDF and will be upgraded for continued service through the 1990s. This pastel-coloured F-4EJ is from 302 Hikotai. *Katsuhiko Tokunaga/KOKU-FAN*

Except for the fact that they lack in-flight refuelling systems and bombing equipment, JASDF F-4EJ Phantoms are similar to USAF F-4Es. This F-4EJ is operated by 301 Hikotai (squadron) at Nyutabaru AB.
Katsuhiko Tokunaga/KOKU-FAN

Japan was the only country to build complete F-4 Phantoms besides the US, actually completing the last Phantoms after the McDonnell Douglas assembly line in St Louis, Mo, closed down. With the support of numerous sub-contractors, Japanese F-4EJ Phantoms were built by Mitsubishi. This F-4EJ is assigned to 302 Hikotai at Naha AB.
Katsuhiko Tokunaga/KOKU-FAN

Making a rapid take-off, this shark-mouthed F-4EJ is from 303 Hikotai at Komatsu AB. The first 13 JASDF F-4EJs were either built in St Louis as pattern aircraft or assembled in Japan from kits supplied by McDonnell Douglas. Once Mitsubishi began producing F-4EJs, orders for the JASDF increased to a total of 140 aeroplanes. *Katsuhiko Tokunaga/KOKU-FAN*

This F-4EJ is assigned to 305 Hikotai at Huakuri AB which, together with 204 Hikotai, forms the 7th Air Wing. However, 204 Hikotai operates the F-15J Eagle which has replaced the F-4EJ in some JASDF squadrons.
Katsuhiko Tokunaga/KOKU-FAN

Replaced by F-15J Eagles in 1987, these 303 Hikotai F-4EJs sported special camouflage schemes for ACM engagements. Both aeroplanes carried F-104J Starfighter silhouettes on the air intake splitter vanes to indicate successes over simulated aggressors.

Katsuhiko Tokunaga/KOKU-FAN

The JASDF also operates 14 RF-4EJ reconnaissance Phantoms that were built by McDonnell Douglas for use by 501 Hikotai at Hyarkuri AB.

Katsuhiko Tokunaga/KOKU-FAN

The 86th TFW at Ramstein AB, West Germany, converted from F-4E Phantoms to F-16C Fighting Falcons in 1986. This particular Phantom, No 69-0264, flew the last operational Phantom mission for the 86th TFW and was subsequently transferred to the 347th TFW at Moody AFB, Ga.
Theo W. van Geffen/IAAP